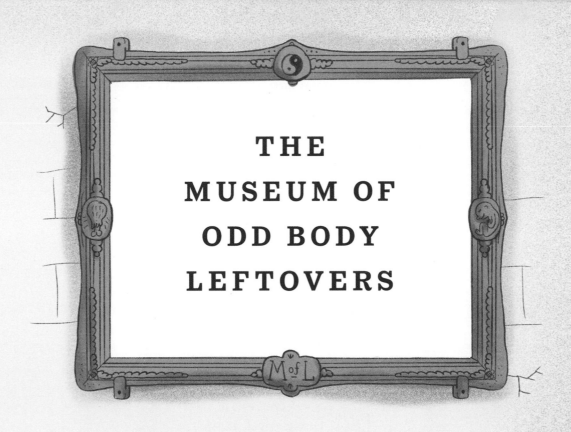

THE
MUSEUM OF
ODD BODY
LEFTOVERS

RACHEL
POLIQUIN

ILLUSTRATIONS BY

Clayton
Hanmer

THE MUSEUM OF Odd BODY LEFTOVERS

A Tour of Your Useless Parts, Flaws, and Other Weird Bits

GREYSTONE KIDS

GREYSTONE BOOKS • VANCOUVER/BERKELEY/LONDON

CONTENTS *MAP*

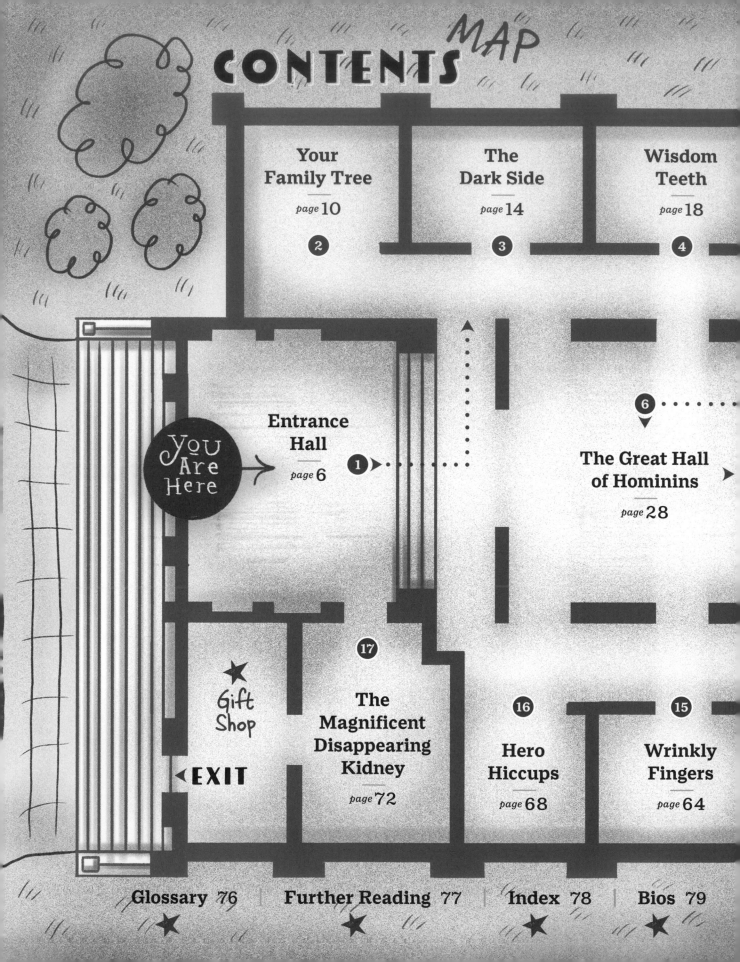

You Are Here

Gift Shop

◄ EXIT

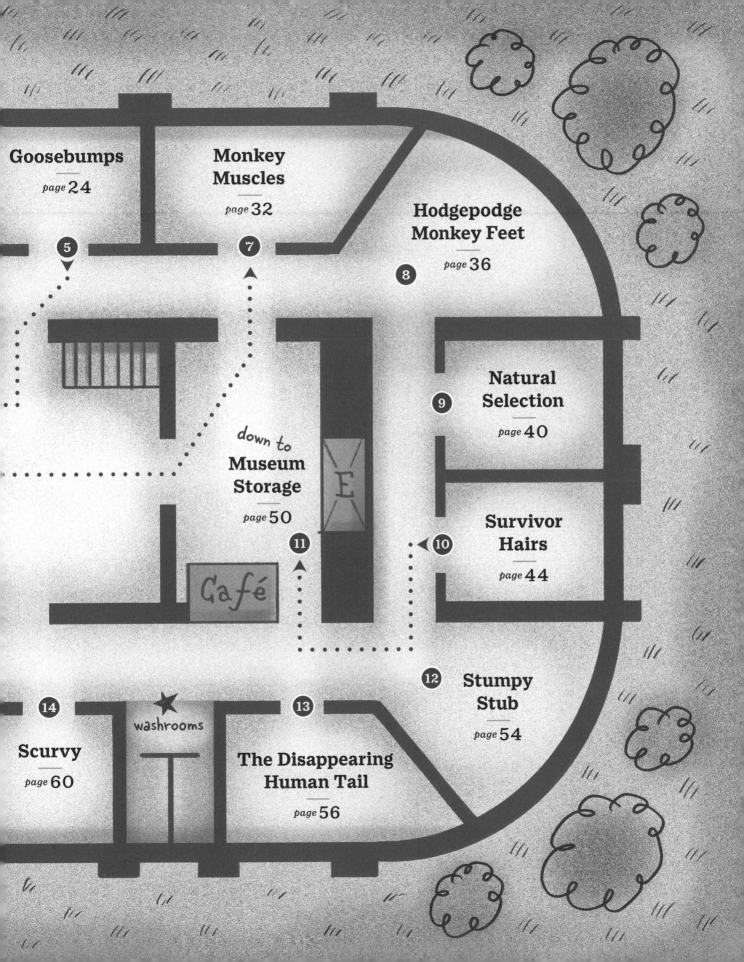

WELCOME TO THE museum *inside* your body! I'm so glad you're here. We have much to talk about!

Of course, you know your body is magnificent and strong. It can run and jump. It has lungs and eyeballs. It can think big thoughts with its great big brain. Wow!

But we're not here to talk about your magnificent parts. We're here to talk about your body's "useless" bits. Yes … you heard right. The useless bits. The leftovers. The bad patch jobs. The weird shrunken parts nobody really uses anymore. Your body has plenty of those too.

And guess what? I'm one of them! I'm not just a tooth. I'm a *Wisdom* Tooth! And that means I am smart and sturdy and can grow so crookedly in your mouth that your dentist has to yank me out.

To be honest, that last part isn't so good for you or me. But don't think it makes me unimportant. Yes, you can live a long and happy life without me, but I am still important. In fact, all of us leftovers are so important and (dare I say it?) downright fabulous that scientists have given us a special name: **vestigial structures.***

*****vestigial structures**
(pronounce it like this)
*ves-TIDGE-gee-al
STRUCK-sures*

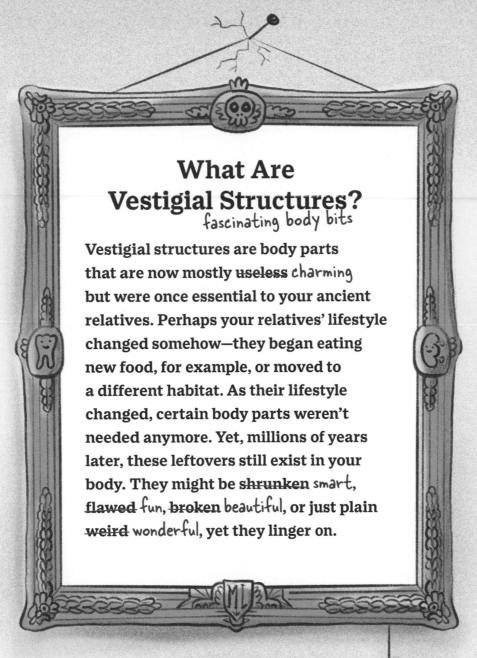

What Are
Vestigial Structures?
fascinating body bits

Vestigial structures are body parts
that are now mostly ~~useless~~ charming
but were once essential to your ancient
relatives. Perhaps your relatives' lifestyle
changed somehow—they began eating
new food, for example, or moved to
a different habitat. As their lifestyle
changed, certain body parts weren't
needed anymore. Yet, millions of years
later, these leftovers still exist in your
body. They might be ~~shrunken~~ smart,
~~flawed~~ fun, ~~broken~~ beautiful, or just plain
~~weird~~ wonderful, yet they linger on.

Why are we so important? Because together
we tell the story of how you became a human.

I don't mean you personally. I mean how all humans
everywhere came to have two legs and two arms and ten
fingers and hair on your head and all the other things that
make you different from a dog or a snake or a palm tree.

You see, humans haven't always been around. A few million years ago, you didn't exist at all. But your **ancestors** did. They were furry and had lovely teeth. And millions and millions of years before that, your ancestors scuttled on four legs like lizards. And even further back, maybe 400 million years ago, all your relatives were fish and lived in the sea. Amazing!

So how do we so-called useless leftovers tell that story? I'm glad you asked!

Welcome to your body—your own personal museum of leftovers, flaws, and other weird bits that have been hanging around since before your ancestors were human.

I, Wisdom Tooth, will be your trusty guide as we wander the halls and travel back in time. Along the way, we'll meet other amazing leftovers like Goosebumps, Wrinkly Fingers, and, most terrifying, Scurvy. (It's a terrible disease—your teeth fall out! Horrors!) I'll also introduce you to some of your earliest relatives from hundreds of millions of years ago.

There's a lot to see and learn. So let's get going. Not a minute to lose!

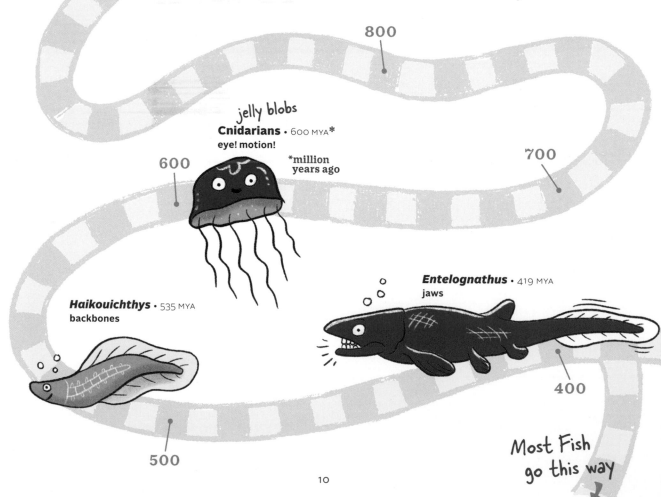

specks of life
Prokaryotes · ~3.8 BYA*
tiny but alive!

*billion
years ago

Before
life began

YOUR FAMILY TREE

L ET ME INTRODUCE YOU to your family. First there were just
tiny one-celled specks of life floating in ancient seas. There
wasn't much more to life on Earth for a long, long time, but about
3 billion years later, things really started to happen. First jelly
blobs. Then sponges and sea-cucumbers. Next came the Age of
Fish—look, one has legs! Then creatures that look like salamanders,
lizards, a cross between an iguana and a badger, a tree shrew, some
monkeys, the apes, and eventually you: *Homo sapiens*. (That's your
official scientific name—the one you share with every other human
on this planet.) And this is the story of how humans came to be.
From jelly blobs to humans in about half a billion years.

800

jelly blobs
Cnidarians · 600 MYA*
eye! motion!

*million
years ago

600

700

Entelognathus · 419 MYA
jaws

Haikouichthys · 535 MYA
backbones

400

500

10

Most Fish
go this way

200

Juramaia · 160 MYA
warm-blooded!

100

the badger–iguana
Thrinaxodon · 240 MYA
fur!

Purgatorius · 65 MYA
almost a monkey

Monkeys
this way

This way to
Humans!

300

Archaeothyris · 306 MYA
lived on land

Proconsul · 28 MYA
no tail!

Hominins · 7 MYA
almost human!

This way to
Amphibians

Tiktaalik · 375 MYA
four "legs"

Of course, this diagram tells the human story, but every living thing has its own story and its own set of ancestors going all the way back to those first tiny specks of life. That means *all animals that ever lived are related*–including you. You're all part of this same enormous family tree and all have at least some ancient ancestors in common.

Ichthyostega · 365 MYA
gills *and* lungs!

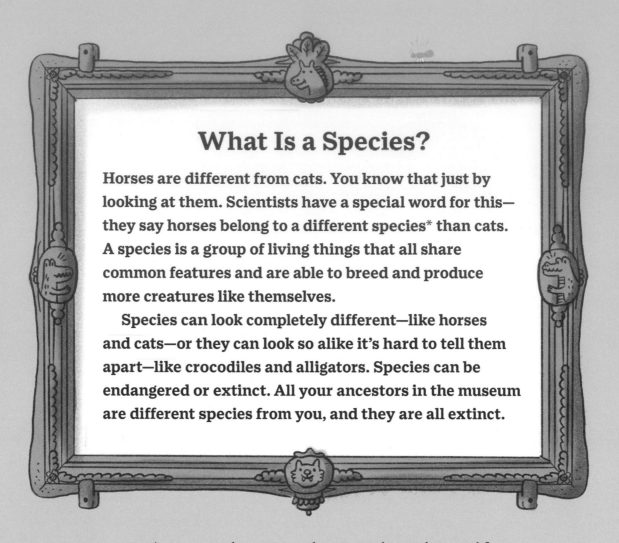

What Is a Species?

Horses are different from cats. You know that just by looking at them. Scientists have a special word for this—they say horses belong to a different species* than cats. A species is a group of living things that all share common features and are able to breed and produce more creatures like themselves.

Species can look completely different—like horses and cats—or they can look so alike it's hard to tell them apart—like crocodiles and alligators. Species can be endangered or extinct. All your ancestors in the museum are different species from you, and they are all extinct.

*species
(pronounce it like this)
SPEE-sees

This is a very big story, and scientists have a big word for it: **evolution**. The process of evolution explains how everything that ever lived on our planet—including worms, dinosaurs, cucumbers, pigeons, and you—came to exist. You see, pigeons didn't just appear one day. Neither did worms. And neither did you. You all *evolved* from other creatures that looked a lot like you, but not quite. In turn, those creatures *evolved* from creatures that looked a lot like them, but not quite. And so on and so on over millions and millions and *millions* of years, with each creature changing just a little bit here and there to become better at living in its environment.

After millions of years of tiny changes, a creature might look very different from its ancestors. And that's what *evolve* really means—to change enough to become a new sort of living thing, or what scientists call a new species. In turn, this new species will change a little bit here and there, over more millions of years, to become something new again.

This is the *official* story of evolution. It's what you'll find in all the science books. It's what biology teachers will teach you and what most grown-ups could explain, more or less.

However, I am going to tell you the other side of this story, the dark side. It isn't as tidy. And it isn't a story of glorious triumph, but it is far more interesting. It's our story. The story of us leftovers—the bits evolution broke, bent, forgot, or shrunk. I know you want to hear it. So step this way.

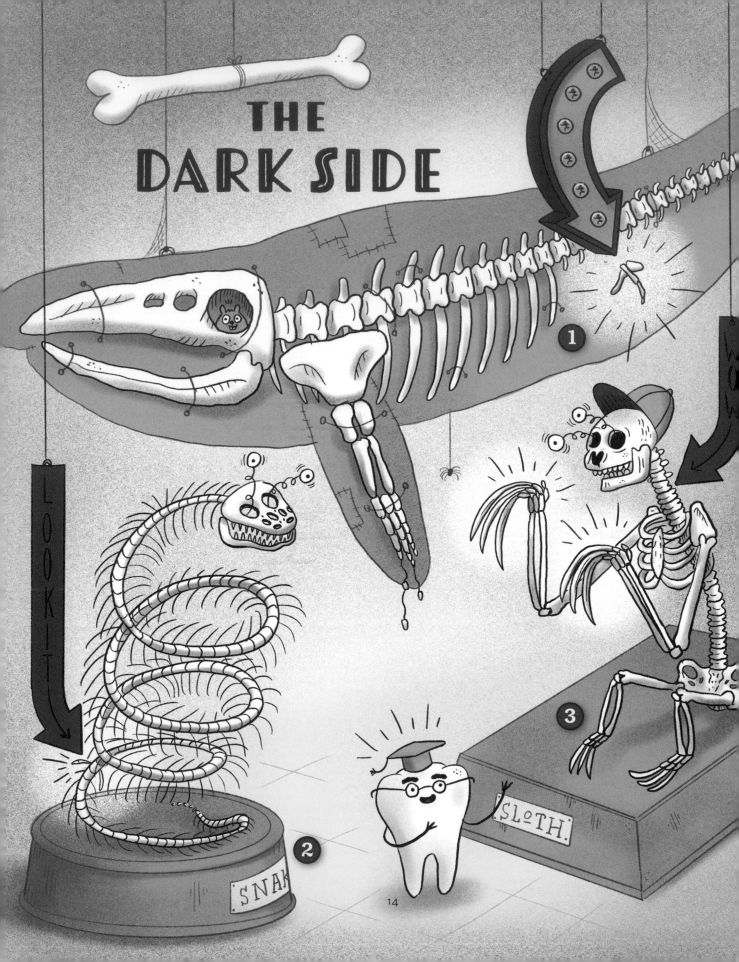

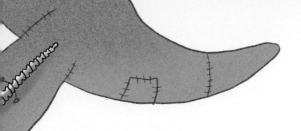

1

WHALE: Millions of years before blue whales existed, their ancestors walked on four legs. Whales still have hip bones from those distant days and sometimes tiny legs.

2

SNAKE: Boa constrictors and pythons often have very small hind legs (really just bumps), leftovers from when their ancient ancestors scrambled on four legs.

3

SLOTH: Three-toed sloths have only three fingers on each hand, but they have extra bones from when their ancestors had five fingers, like you.

Science books always describe evolution as a wonderful process filled with new species and new skills and new lifestyles. But there's a dark side to all this newness.

When a creature evolves into a new species, it's often because that creature started doing something different, or maybe its world became different. Maybe it discovered some very tasty, crunchy nuts. Or maybe the climate cooled, and nights turned chilly. After millions of years of trying to survive or make the most of these changes, the creature's great-great-grandchildren might look very different. They might have bigger teeth for crunching nuts or huge fur coats for warmth.

Scientists call these body bits **traits**. The bigger teeth and fur coats are traits that help the animals live longer, happier, healthier lives in their changing world.

But what about the bits the animals had *before*? Like maybe while the climate was hot, the animal fanned itself with giant ears. Or maybe the nut-eater licked up ants with a long tongue. Big air-conditioning ears aren't useful in the cold, and long tongues don't help with crunchy nuts. So what happens to these traits? *What happens to the leftovers?* This, my friends, is the dark side of evolution.

Some lucky leftovers find a new and useful role—like maybe the animal will use its enormous ears as blankets. Some leftovers vanish like ghosts, *as if they were never there*. But the rest of us just linger on. Maybe we shrink or shrivel. Mostly, we hang around not doing much of anything for millions and millions of years. It doesn't feel great. I would like to be useful. But now you're here, and I can tell you our story!

Look, our first room. And it's a good one!

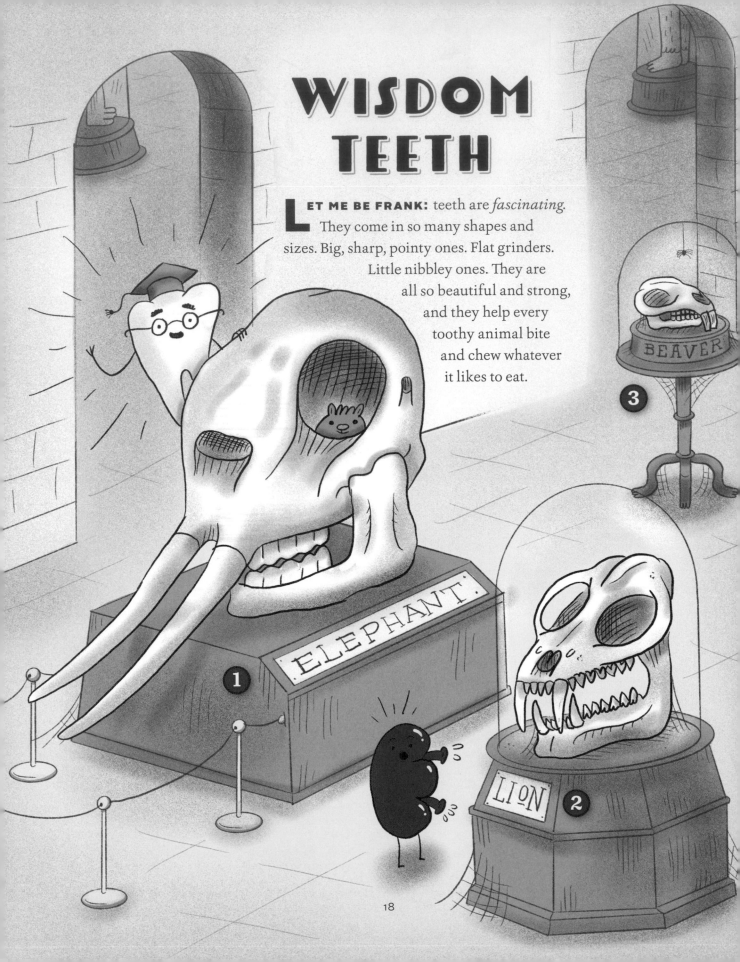

WISDOM TEETH

LET ME BE FRANK: teeth are *fascinating*. They come in so many shapes and sizes. Big, sharp, pointy ones. Flat grinders. Little nibbley ones. They are all so beautiful and strong, and they help every toothy animal bite and chew whatever it likes to eat.

ELEPHANT **1**

LION **2**

BEAVER **3**

18

ELEPHANT
Loxodonta africana
Enormous molar for grinding tough plants

LION
Panthera leo
Long, pointy canine teeth for grabbing and tearing meat

BEAVER
Castor canadensis
Sharp incisors at the front for cutting; molars at the back for chewing

What about *your* teeth? I don't know how old you are, so I don't know exactly how many teeth you have. Babies usually don't have any. If you're between two and five, you probably have 20 lovely teeth—these ones are called your baby teeth, or **milk teeth**.

Around age six, you start to lose them. One by one they fall out, and brand-new, shiny-white teeth grow in their place—you get to keep these ones your whole life. And it gets better! You'll also start to get adult **molars**. These are big, broad, flat-topped teeth at the back of your jaws, especially designed for serious chewing. By the time you're nine, you'll have 4. Around age fourteen, you'll get another 4. And by age twenty-five, you'll probably have 4 more, for a grand total of 32 adult teeth including 12 amazing molars!

These last 4 are the special ones. They're my brothers and sisters: the Wisdom Teeth! Some say we're called **wisdom teeth** because we don't appear until you're an adult, by which time you are supposed to be wise. But I think it's because we make you wise. Either way, we wise guys at the back can cause big trouble.

Sometimes we grow completely sideways and shove your other teeth around. Sometimes we grow into your jawbone and cause terrible pain. Sometimes dentists just pull us out before we get the chance to make a mess.

Early Farming

But this bad behavior isn't *our* fault. It's your fault! Your adult jaws aren't big enough to fit us, which is absurd! Look inside the mouth of any other animal—you won't find a single jaw too small for its teeth. Some animals replace their teeth throughout their lives, like sharks. Some have ever-growing teeth, like beavers. But humans are the only animals that can't fit all their teeth in their mouths!

Even you humans didn't have this problem until very recently in your long history. In fact, you only need to go back about 14,000 years to find human jaws with plenty of room for all 32 teeth.

So what happened?

Humans quit hard chewing! Can you believe it?!

It all started when your early ancestors began collecting wild seeds and sowing them as crops. They collected the grains, ground them into flour, and cooked the flour into porridge and soft breads. All this mush spelled doom for my family.

Farming and Cooking

Around 10,000 years ago, in an area in the Middle East now known as the Fertile Crescent, humans began gathering wild seeds and sowing them as crops. Before, humans mainly hunted meat and gathered fruits, nuts, and wild tubers to eat, which meant they had to move often to find food. Farming allowed them to settle in one place, store food, and build villages.

ruin their mouths
with mush,

You see, before humans started farming and cooking mush, they gathered nuts and ate stringy meat and tough roots. They needed good teeth, solid jawbones, and strong jaw muscles. Jaw muscles are like any muscles; the more you use them, the bigger they get. The same is true of jaw*bones*. If kids only eat super-tough foods, the stress of hard chewing makes their jawbones grow thicker and stronger and *longer*. The more they chew, the bigger their jaws get.

So here's the problem: you don't need big, long, strong jaws to eat scrambled eggs and waffles, and that's why human jawbones aren't growing to their full potential. And that's why you humans can't fit all your teeth in your mouth anymore.

But there is hope. Scientists say that if kids chew tough and stringy jerky all day every day, their jaws might grow big enough to fit all 32 teeth. You're a kid—do you want to try? I didn't think so.

And so this is why I'm in the Museum of Odd Body Leftovers. Your chewing habits changed, and suddenly you didn't need me anymore. But just because you don't need me doesn't mean I disappear. As I said before, we leftovers can hang around for millions of years and more.

Next up, the thousands of tiny muscles in your skin. Scientists call them the arrector pili muscles, but I call them Goosebumps Galore!

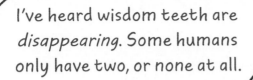

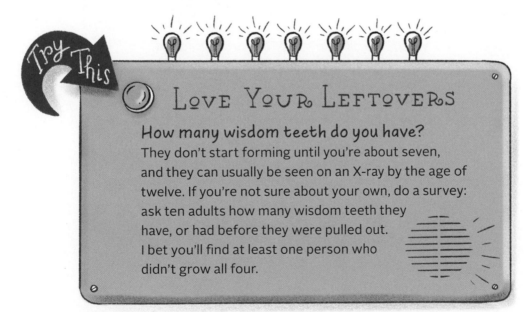

LOVE YOUR LEFTOVERS

How many wisdom teeth do you have?
They don't start forming until you're about seven, and they can usually be seen on an X-ray by the age of twelve. If you're not sure about your own, do a survey: ask ten adults how many wisdom teeth they have, or had before they were pulled out. I bet you'll find at least one person who didn't grow all four.

GOOSEBUMPS

Winter in the Spooky Forest

GOOSEBUMPS. You know all about them. When you're cold or scared or listening to beautiful music, you get little bumps all over your body and your hairs stick straight up.

Do you know why? It is because you're a **mammal**, and mammals are famously furry. Humans aren't furry anymore, but you are still mammals, and your bodies still work as if they were furry.

Let me explain with this fox. When a fox gets chilly, muscles around each of its hairs tighten so the hairs stand straight up. This makes a little space between the fox's skin and the tip of the hairs. Heat from the fox's body warms the air inside that space, and the thick fur prevents the warm air from escaping. The whole puffy system keeps the fox super cozy. It's sort of like putting on a sweater under your winter jacket.

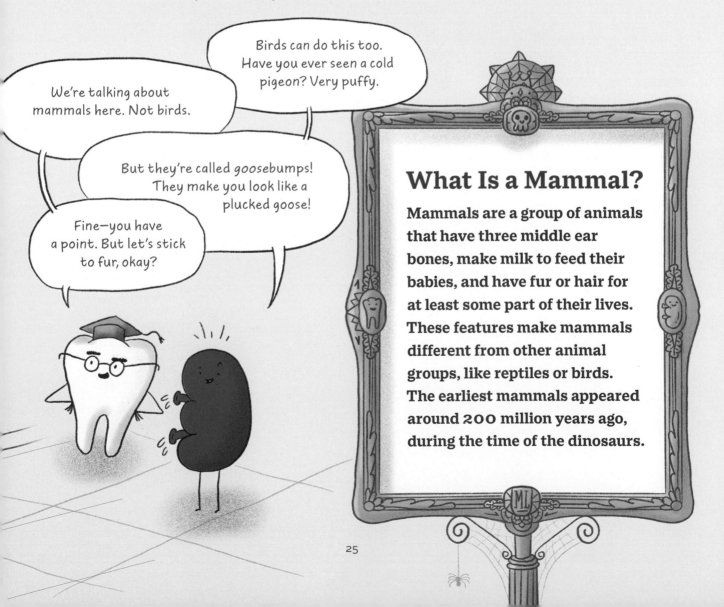

Birds can do this too. Have you ever seen a cold pigeon? Very puffy.

We're talking about mammals here. Not birds.

But they're called *goosebumps!* They make you look like a plucked goose!

Fine—you have a point. But let's stick to fur, okay?

What Is a Mammal?

Mammals are a group of animals that have three middle ear bones, make milk to feed their babies, and have fur or hair for at least some part of their lives. These features make mammals different from other animal groups, like reptiles or birds. The earliest mammals appeared around 200 million years ago, during the time of the dinosaurs.

The same thing can happen when an animal is afraid or surprised. Have you ever seen a spooked cat or snarling dog? Its fur stands up to make it look bigger and fiercer.

Evolution stole your fur, but did your goosebump muscles give up? Of course not! They may be little, but they're feisty! When you get cold or have strong emotions, they get to work and make your survivor hairs stand as straight as they ever did on a fox. You don't have enough hairs to create a cozy layer or make you look huge and fierce. But those brave little muscles keep working despite all the obstacles evolution has thrown in their way.

All growing human babies are completely furry. And then—abracadabra!—the fur disappears before the babies are born.

You love talking about disappearing.

Of course I do! I am a Disappearing Kidney!

I don't know about babies before they are born, but I do know some babies are born covered in soft fuzz. It's called **lanugo**.*

Yes, Tooth. And even that disappears within a few weeks.

*lanugo
(pronounce it like this)
lah-NEW-go

26

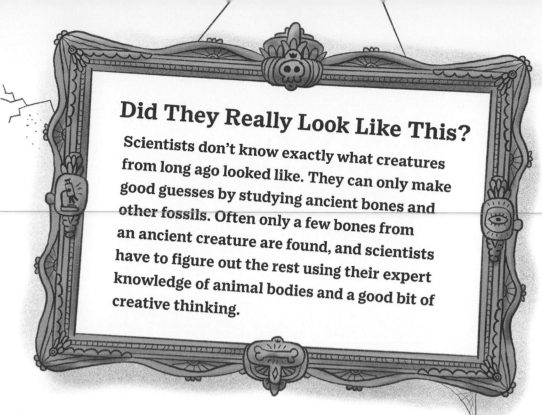

Did They Really Look Like This?

Scientists don't know exactly what creatures from long ago looked like. They can only make good guesses by studying ancient bones and other fossils. Often only a few bones from an ancient creature are found, and scientists have to figure out the rest using their expert knowledge of animal bodies and a good bit of creative thinking.

So why *did* evolution take your fur? Fur is a wonderful thing. It's warm. It protects your skin. It's gorgeous and silky soft. It can be patterned with spots and stripes for **camouflage**.* A few million years ago, your ancestors had lovely fur. You look plucked and naked without it. What happened?

To be honest, I'm not 100 percent sure. But look—the Great Hall of Hominins! I'm sure we'll find some answers in there.

camouflage
(pronounce it like this)
CAM-*oh-flahzh*

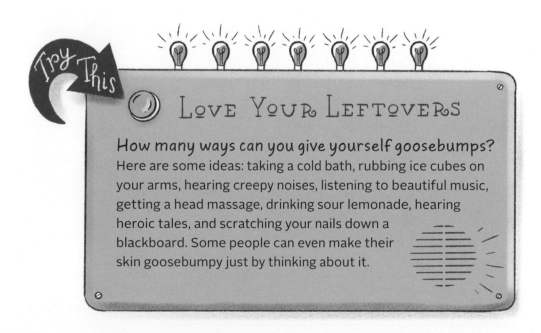

Try This

Love Your Leftovers

How many ways can you give yourself goosebumps? Here are some ideas: taking a cold bath, rubbing ice cubes on your arms, hearing creepy noises, listening to beautiful music, getting a head massage, drinking sour lemonade, hearing heroic tales, and scratching your nails down a blackboard. Some people can even make their skin goosebumpy just by thinking about it.

The GREAT HALL OF HOMININS

WELCOME TO
The Great Hall of Hominins!
There are so many of them—at least
20 species and maybe more. **Hominins***
are a special group in your family tree.
They include all humans that ever
lived and all your human-like ancestors.

These particular hominins may not be
your ancestors—scientists are still figuring
out how they all fit together. But your
ancestors probably looked
a lot like them.

***hominins**
(pronounce it like this)
HOM-uh-nins

Ardi

Lucy

hAirY JiM

1 — Ardipithecus ramidus

3 — Homo erectus

2 — Australopithecus afarensis

1
aka Ardi
Ardipithecus ramidus
5–4 MYA | 4 feet tall
Ardi had long arms and a grasping big toe for climbing, like a chimpanzee. Her hips and stiffer feet allowed her to walk upright on the ground.

2
aka Lucy
Australopithecus afarensis
4–3 MYA | 3.5 feet tall
Lucy had long arms and curved fingers for climbing, while her thigh bones and arched feet were built for walking on two legs.

3
aka Hairy Jim
Homo erectus
1.8–0.1 MYA | up to 6 feet tall
Homo erectus means "upright human," and this ancestor was bigger, faster, smarter, and more like you than any other hominin before it.

You can guess a little about the lives of these hominins, just by their bodies. Ardi's long arms and bendy feet were great for swinging and hanging from branches. Lucy's feet were better for walking on the ground, but she probably spent time in trees too. (Scientists think she made night nests for safety.) And then there's Hairy Jim. He looked a lot like your average human, but hairier. His legs and feet were built for running, and his arms weren't any bigger than your gym teacher's.

Why Walk When You Can Swing?

Why did your ancestors leave the safety of trees? One theory suggests Earth's climate went through a series of hot and cold cycles. During hot cycles, jungles grew lush and filled with fruit. During cold and dry cycles, forests shrank, grasslands grew, and competition for food became fierce.

Maybe your ancestors were pushed out of the shrinking forests by bigger apes. Maybe they had to walk between forests for food. Maybe they wanted to carry a spear, a baby, or a basket of fruit. Or maybe standing helped them see danger in the distance. No one really knows for sure.

WELCOME · TO YOUR INNER MONKEY

This is the basic story of human evolution: your early ape-like ancestors mostly lived in trees. Then, over a few million years, your ancestors spent more and more time on the ground until they never went back. No one really knows why. But whatever the reason, it was a very big lifestyle change.

Think of tree-living animals, like sloths, orangutans, and koalas. They are built differently than grassland animals. Their hands and feet are made for climbing and hanging, not walking or running. As your ancestors began to live on the ground, their bodies had to change to survive. Their feet stiffened and lost their bendiness—that helped them walk on the ground. They lost their monkey toes. Their arms shrank. Their fur disappeared. But don't despair—you still have lots of monkey leftovers. In fact, this whole next wing of the museum is dedicated to Your Inner Monkey.

MONKEY MUSCLES

YOU CAN'T DO half the tricks monkeys can, but you still have monkey muscles—at least some of you. You might have a small muscle in your forearm, left over from when your monkey ancestors walked on all fours. Scientists call it the palmaris longus. About one in five people don't have it. It's so tiny, it doesn't make any difference to your strength.

Do I have it?

Don't be ridiculous! You're a kidney. You don't even have arms.

Nacholapithecus kerioi

You also have the skinniest muscle in your calf. Scientists call this one the plantaris. It's probably left over from when your feet could grip branches. One in ten people don't have it, and it doesn't make any difference to your leg strength either. Even I can't pretend these muscles are interesting.

Much more interesting is some monkey muscle power you had as a baby. When human babies are born, they have super strength in their hands: the Monkey Grip! And I'm not talking about special babies. I'm talking about regular newborns that can't smile or roll over or scratch their noses. These basic baby blobs have such a powerful grip, they can dangle from a rope using just one hand! It's incredible! Within a few months, the power disappears, but at the beginning of life, your inner monkey is strong!

aka Nacho
Nacholapithecus kerioi
This early ape lived about 15 million years ago in Kenya. It had no tail, long feet, large arms, and mobile shoulders for swinging—all features of modern apes. Humans likely descended from an ape that looked a lot like ~~this one~~. Nacho

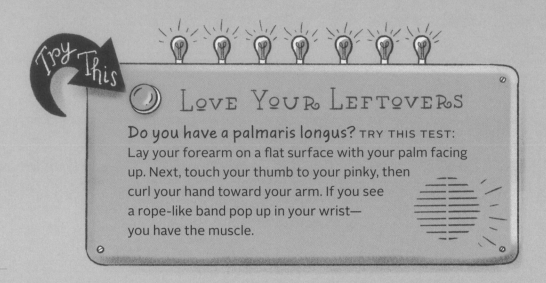

Try This

LOVE YOUR LEFTOVERS

Do you have a palmaris longus? TRY THIS TEST:
Lay your forearm on a flat surface with your palm facing
up. Next, touch your thumb to your pinky, then
curl your hand toward your arm. If you see
a rope-like band pop up in your wrist—
you have the muscle.

Scientists call this grip and grasp the palmar reflex.
A **reflex** is something your body does without you having
to think about it. Goosebumps are also a reflex—your muscles
react to cold and tighten on their own. It's the same with the
palmar reflex; babies aren't thinking, "I must hold tight with
my tiny fists." Their hands just grab and hold whatever touches
their palm. Scientists think it's a leftover from when your baby
ancestors clung to their mothers' fur and held on tight as the
moms climbed and swung through the forest.

And here's another super-weird monkey-muscle leftover: the
Big Twitch. Has your body ever jerked suddenly, just as you were
about to fall asleep? That jerk might have stopped your ancient
relatives from tumbling out of trees! Some scientists think the
Big Twitch would snap sleepy monkeys awake, so they could
safely position themselves in their tree before falling asleep
for the night.

Next up, your feet. Obviously, your feet aren't
leftovers—you use them every day. But evolution
did a pretty ridiculous patch job on them.

HODGEPODGE MONKEY FEET

DID YOU KNOW ostriches are super sprinters and the world's fastest marathon runners? Yet they never twist an ankle. Or tear an **Achilles tendon**.* Or get sore feet. Do you know why?

Because *T. rex* is their great-granddaddy.

Well, *Tyrannosaurus rex* isn't their direct ancestor, but both *T. rex* and ostriches are part of an ancient group of creatures known as **theropods*** that all walked on two legs. The first theropods lived around 230 million years ago, and ever since, all theropods—including *T. rex*, velociraptors, and every bird that has ever lived—have walked on two legs. In other words, *for more than 230 million years* birds and their ancestors have been two-legged runners. For humans, it's been about 4 million years. That is a very large difference in time.

What's interesting is that you and birds are the only animals that run on two feet. Sure, dogs and bears can walk on their hind legs for a bit, but it's really only birds and humans who are officially and properly **bipedal**,* which is a fancy way of saying "two-legged-walking." Yet your feet and bird feet could not be more different.

*Achilles tendon
(pronounce it like this)
*ah-KILL-lees
TEN-don*

*theropods
(pronounce it like this)
THER-uh-pods

*bipedal
(pronounce it like this)
BAI-pee-dal

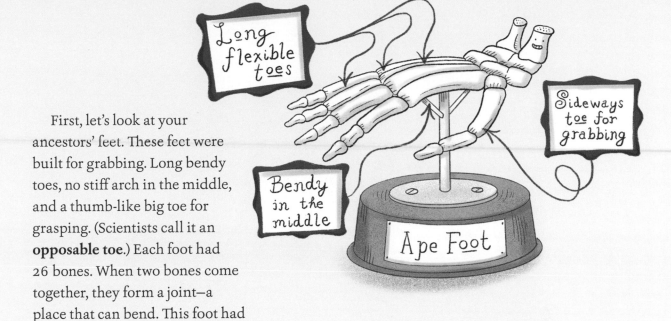

First, let's look at your ancestors' feet. These feet were built for grabbing. Long bendy toes, no stiff arch in the middle, and a thumb-like big toe for grasping. (Scientists call it an **opposable toe**.) Each foot had 26 bones. When two bones come together, they form a joint—a place that can bend. This foot had 33 joints, which made for super flexibility in every direction. It was the perfect foot for grasping branches or holding mangoes.

Next, let's look at an ostrich foot. These feet are built for ground speed. Each foot has a giant big toe for pushing off with power, a terrifying claw for gripping the ground, and *nine bones*. That's it—nine bones! Fewer bones mean fewer joints and less flexibility *but* more stability and strength. It's the perfect runner's foot. In fact, when scientists design **prosthetic*** feet for runners who don't have legs, they use ostriches as their model. Strength, spring, stability—they have it all.

***prosthetic**
(pronounce it like this)
pross-THET-tic

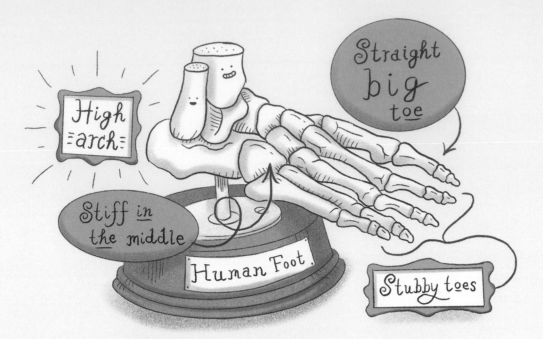

High arch

Straight big toe

Stiff in the middle

Human Foot

Stubby toes

Now for your feet. You run, which means your feet must be stiff and springy, like an ostrich's. Yet a few million years ago your ancestors had super-flexible, floppy monkey feet. How does that work? Well, it doesn't, unless evolution gets wacky. What you have is a floppy monkey foot held stiff with tape and paper clips. Not really, but you get the idea.

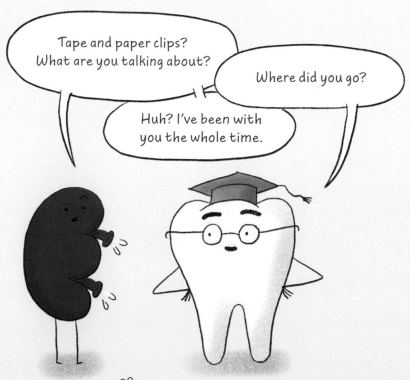

Tape and paper clips? What are you talking about?

Where did you go?

Huh? I've been with you the whole time.

You see, your foot still has all 26 bones and 33 joints for super flexibility. *But* evolution has also given you more than 100 muscles and tendons to hold all those joints straight enough for you to push off in a run. As you can probably imagine, a bunch of little foot bones stuck together will never be as strong as one big bone—like what the ostrich has. That's why humans are famous for sprained ankles, torn tendons, hammertoes, and all the other foot problems that come with your Hodgepodge Monkey Feet.

No one would design such a foot, if they could build it from scratch. However, building from scratch is very, very hard—even for evolution. It takes hundreds of millions of mistakes over hundreds of millions of years to build something new. Evolution mostly just shapes and pulls and twists and shrinks what is already there.

But how? How does a tree-climbing foot become a running foot? How *do* bodies change? This is a very big question. Time to roll up my sleeves and give you a big answer. Are you ready?

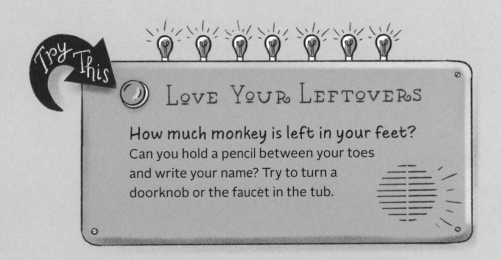

Try This

Love Your Leftovers

How much monkey is left in your feet?
Can you hold a pencil between your toes and write your name? Try to turn a doorknob or the faucet in the tub.

NATURAL SELECTION

HOW DID YOUR ancestors go from climbing trees to running marathons? It happens by something I call "Little Differences, Big Changes." It goes like this:

No two living things are *exactly* the same, even though they might look *mostly* the same. Like you and your friend—you are both human. But one of you has longer legs or bigger feet or darker hair or any of the innumerable tiny differences that make each of us unique. Scientists call this **genetic variation***— it just means we are all a bit different. And those little genetic differences can explain big changes.

Let's say millions of years ago, a few of your ancestors had *slightly* stiffer feet than their friends, which meant they had a slightly better chance of outrunning a lion or walking far enough to find better berries. That gave them a slightly better chance of surviving long enough to have slightly stiffer-footed children. In turn, those children might have even stiffer-footed children and grandchildren, who might have even better chances of surviving. At the same time, the slightly floppier-footed friends had a slightly worse chance with the lions. And so on and so on over millions of years.

***genetic variation**
(pronounce it like this)
juh-NET-ic
very-ay-shun

This movie is sooo slow.

I'm going to need more popcorn.

40

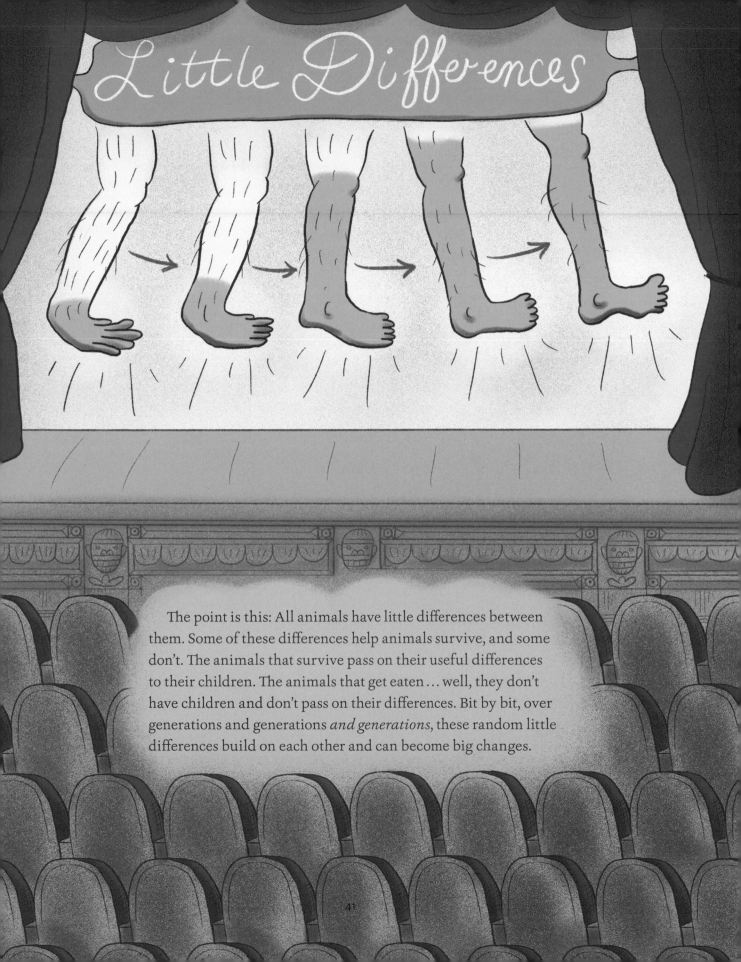

Little Differences

The point is this: All animals have little differences between them. Some of these differences help animals survive, and some don't. The animals that survive pass on their useful differences to their children. The animals that get eaten... well, they don't have children and don't pass on their differences. Bit by bit, over generations and generations *and generations*, these random little differences build on each other and can become big changes.

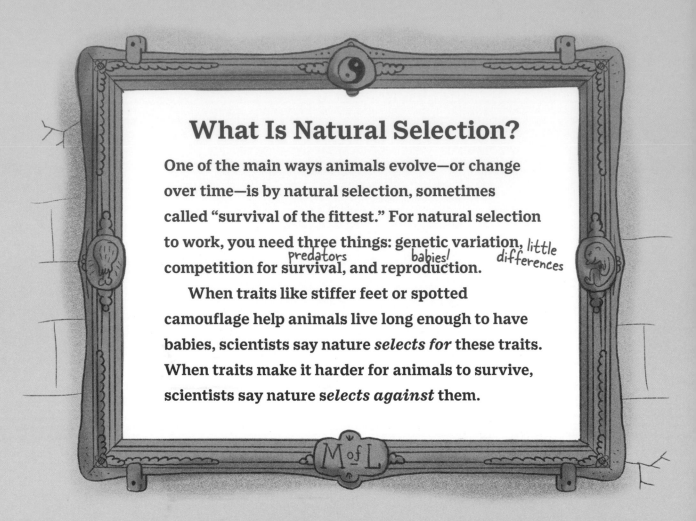

What Is Natural Selection?

One of the main ways animals evolve—or change over time—is by natural selection, sometimes called "survival of the fittest." For natural selection to work, you need three things: genetic variation, *little differences* competition for survival, and reproduction. *predators* *babies!*

When traits like stiffer feet or spotted camouflage help animals live long enough to have babies, scientists say nature *selects for* these traits. When traits make it harder for animals to survive, scientists say nature s*elects against* them.

And that's how human feet changed. As early humans spent more and more time on the ground, stiffer and springier feet worked better than flexible, floppy feet. And since stiffer and stiffer feet worked better and better over millions and millions of generations, those with the stiffest feet triumphed in their new grassland environment. Scientists call this theory **natural selection**.

Natural selection is *not* random—there's a reason some animals get eaten and others don't. However, the little differences *are* random. Why did some apes have slightly stiffer feet? It was just a random little difference, like the differences between you and your friend. Sometimes these random little differences turn out to be *advantageous*—which is a fancy word for a really good thing.

But a really good thing for whom? As new species evolve, old species go extinct. In fact, of all the species that have ever lived on this planet, 99.9 percent of them are extinct. Gone! Disappeared! Sure, millions of creatures died during terrible times, like when an asteroid hit the Earth 66 million years ago. But way more species have disappeared because of evolution.

Yet everyone *loves* evolution. They admire all the new body parts and completely forget about the old, not-so-useful bits. But evolution doesn't forget them. While everyone is admiring the new, evolution is busily shrinking the old, squishing the useless, and trying to shrivel us leftovers into nothingness. Like your fur— what *did* happen to your fur?

SURVIVOR HAIRS

YOUR BODY HAIRS might be nearly invisible or thick like a carpet, but you all have at least some survivor hairs from when you were super furry.

If you ask a scientist why you lost your fur, she'll probably tell you that being less furry must have been *useful* to your ancestors. But how? And why? Scientists can't quite agree yet, but they have lots of ideas.

Faster. Farther. Nakeder.

The SWEATY RUNNER

• On display now •

THEORY #1
The Sweaty Runner

As humans began running faster on their stiffer feet, they were getting hot. Running is sweaty work, especially in a fur coat. Maybe less fur helped them run faster (away from lions) and farther (to get better food) without overheating. Humans also have a weirdly large number of sweat glands. More sweat glands means more sweat, which means rapid cooling. The combo of less fur and more sweat glands may have helped your ancestors run and hunt longer, even in the midday heat.

THEORY #2
The Hot Brain

Humans have enormous brains, and big brains make a lot of heat. Maybe less hair kept bodies cool enough to grow enormous, hot brains. That doesn't explain why you have hair on your head, but keeping your head furry does prevent sunburns up top.

THEORY #3
Less Is More

Maybe your ancestors thought less hair was pretty and choose mates who were less furry.

This is called **sexual selection** or "survival of the beautiful." It works just like natural selection (with little differences adding up to big changes over time), except only the beautiful are chosen to have children. Only the animals with prettiest feathers or biggest antlers pass on their beautiful difference.

THEORY #4
Bug Begone

Less hair meant fewer bugs.
Maybe humans with less fur
were healthier.

THEORY #5
The Watery Ape

I've been told this theory is definitely *not
true*. Yet it's too much fun not to tell. This
theory says that some of your monkey
ancestors lived in water, like whales.
That's why humans have so much fat and
so few hairs, just like whales. The Watery
Ape theory also explains why humans
cry salt tears, get pruney fingers in water,
have long head hair (it's for babies to grip),
why babies know to hold their breath
underwater… the list goes on. But as I say,
I've been told this is definitely not true.

THEORY #6

Bad Balding

Yet another theory argues that losing your fur was not a good thing at all, and it didn't happen bit by bit over time. This theory says something weird and wrong happened that caused humans to go mostly bald. Losing fur was *not* advantageous—it was bad and dangerous. What did babies hold on to? How did they stay warm? Early humans just had to make the best of it.

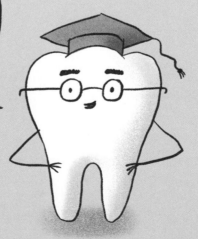

Which theory is true? Or could more than one be true? Don't ask me. It's pretty hard to know why, when, and how humans lost their fur, when scientists only have old bones to look at.

Charles Darwin
(1809-1882)
Charles Darwin was a famous English naturalist, best known for writing the book *On the Origin of Species* (1859), which describes how evolution happens by natural selection. Darwin also explained how vestigial structures are ~~leftovers~~ of such evolutionary change.
charming survivors
Are you going to drink *all* of that?
I'm a kidney— I need to keep hydrated.
I still don't understand why you are here. Without kidneys, humans would die! Kidneys are not leftovers.
I know. Kidneys are fabulous!
The sign says we should go that way.
You can push the button.
Well . . . okay.
to Museum Storage
MORE MONKEY LEFTOVERS This Way

Safety Goggles

You know the little pink blob in the corner of your eye? It's a leftover from your third eyelid. These extra eyelids didn't close up and down, like the eyelids you still have, but side to side. And they were transparent. That means your ancestors could see through them when they were closed—like built-in goggles.

Scientists call them nictitating membranes,* and most bony animals (except most fish) still have them. Swimming animals use them to see underwater without getting grit in their eyeballs. Camels close them during sandstorms. Polar bears use them as sunglasses. Woodpeckers use them as shock absorbers during high-speed pecking.

Why humans lost theirs is ~~a mystery.~~ sad and terrible

*nictitating membranes
(pronounce it like this)
NICK-*tuh-tay-ting*
MEM-*brains*

So many magnificent leftovers!

I don't think we're supposed to be down here.

51

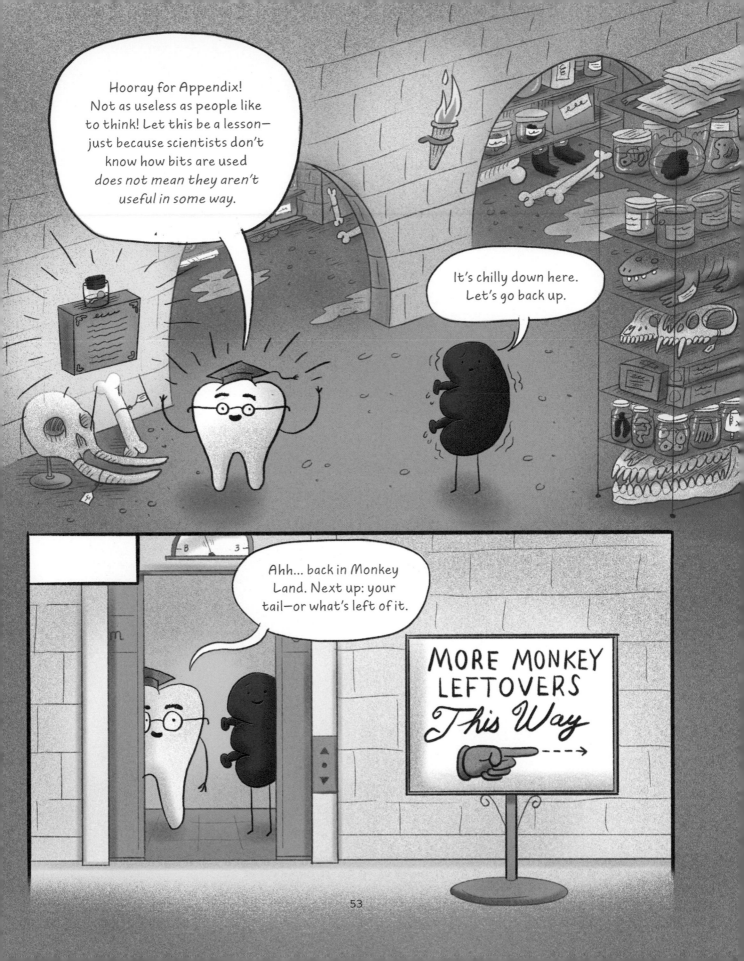

STUMPY STUB

① *Proconsul* | 29–11 MYA
With no tail, long arms, and nimble hands and feet, *Proconsul* might be your last common ancestor with gorillas, orangutans, and the other great apes.

② aka Eggy
Aegyptopithecus | 38–29 MYA
This animal might be the last common ancestor of apes and Old World monkeys, before your ape ancestors split from the monkey branch of the family tree.

SCIENTISTS HAVE discovered the bones of ancient monkeys with long tails, like ~~*Aegyptopithecus*~~, Eggy and the bones of more recent apes without tails, like *Proconsul*. They have yet to find the bones of any creature that fills the gap between long-tailed and no-tailed ancestors. It's a **missing link**!

What's the easiest way to tell an ape from a monkey? No tail! Apes don't have tails while almost all monkeys do. But you and the other apes still have a stubby tail stump. It's called your tailbone or **coccyx**.* It's three to five bones at the bottom of your spine, and it's all that's left of your ancestors' long and lovely tails.

*coccyx
(pronounce it like this)
COK-sicks

54

Why did apes lose their tails? No one really knows, but scientists think ape shoulders might hold a clue. You see, that's another big difference between apes and monkeys—most monkeys can't swing from their arms. Their shoulders don't move that way. Instead, monkeys run along branches on all fours and jump between trees, no swinging required. Long tails really help with that sort of balancing, but they make it harder to balance when you're standing more upright, like most apes. Also, tails are heavy. Who needs extra weight when you spend your days doing the "ape bars"? You probably call them monkey bars, but you shouldn't. Most monkeys couldn't twist their shoulders enough to swing between the bars. Only humans and the other apes can do that.

You know, all humans still grow long and beautiful tails. Then they disappear.

Yes, they do. And I can show you. Step this way.

You and your talk of disappearing! Humans do not grow disappearing tails!

coccyx

Human

The Disappearing Human Tail

ALLOW ME TO explain to you the very true story of the Disappearing Human Tail.

As you may know, all human babies start out tinier than the tiniest kernel of corn. Then they grow and grow inside their mothers. They sprout legs and arms and noses until they look like proper little humans.

From corn kernel to baby takes 280 days, or thereabouts. An astonishing 280 days of constant growing! With each new day comes a new hair, another drop of blood, a more impeccably perfect toenail. Building a baby takes timing and talent— different parts grow at different times, and at exactly the right times. It's like an extraordinary act on the flying trapeze, where every flip and wave is perfectly timed, every catch and spin more difficult,

> A growing baby is nothing like a trapeze act.

> Shush. I'm not finished.

Kernel ~vs.~ baby

Shark

Lizard

Rat

Rabbit

Calf

Tortoise

HUMAN MONSTER!

Unbelievable!

Kernel... Knob... Sausage

AMAZING

Tail

ALIVE

poof!

GONE

salamander

Fish

Human Tail!

every somersault building the excitement, the tension, the grandeur—until the breathtakingly impossible finale! Ta-da!

If you look here, you'll see our kernel grows quickly. Soon the kernel is a knob. The knob becomes a sausage. And then, miracle of miracles, that sausage has a lumpy head, four stubby limbs, a backbone, and, yes—a tail!

The tail is actually part of the backbone, and the backbone—as I'm sure you know—is a very important part of the human body. It's the row of little bones running right down the middle of your back. Now, as the baby grows bigger, so does its tail. The tail grows and grows, longer and longer, until it has 10 to 12 bones, which is fewer than a cat's tail and more than a bear's. Astonishing!

And then, once the whole backbone is perfectly complete from the top of the baby's neck to the tip of its jaunty tail, the extra tail bones make their exit. Their part in the performance is done. They take a bow and dissolve into the background. And there you have it, my friend. The miraculous Disappearing Human Tail!

That's ridiculous! Why grow something and then make it disappear?

It's not at all ridiculous! As I said, every bit and piece of a growing baby has a role in the grand performance. The tail isn't a separate act—it's part of the backbone. And the backbone's role is most especially important. It keeps animals straight and lets them move, bend, and walk. Without a backbone, animals can only slink along like slugs. In other words, mess with the backbone *while it's being built* and the whole show could fall apart. It's much less risky to shorten the backbone *after* the whole thing is built than to snip and tinker *while* it's under construction. It really is just like an act on the flying trapeze—you can't suddenly decide to take a somersault out *during* the performance. It would be a disaster!

Your world is weird. Ooh, look. Scurvy! There's something I know a lot about!

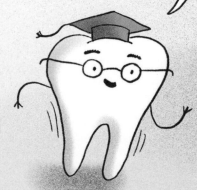

SCURVY

I ONCE HEARD a story about a man who only ate meat and potatoes for a year and *all his teeth fell out.* Awfulness! It was because he didn't eat fruit and didn't get enough vitamin C.

I'm sure your parents are always telling you to eat your fruits and vegetables to get your vitamins and minerals, to eat your meats or other proteins to build muscles, and to drink your milk or milk substitutes to get calcium for strong bones. You have to eat so many different foods to stay healthy.

But what about cows? They only eat grass. How do they get enough protein? Lions only eat meat—no veggies for them. How do these animals get all they need? Why don't their teeth fall out?

Weirdly, these animals don't have to *eat* their vitamins; their bodies can *make* them. By just eating grass or zebras, cows and lions can make every vitamin, mineral, and protein they need to survive. It's amazing!

Actually, it's normal. You humans are the weird ones. But you're not the only ones.

Millions of years ago, some of your ancient ancestors lost their ability to make certain essential vitamins and minerals, and ever since, none of their **descendants*** have been able to either—which means if you don't eat them, you'll become sick. Not enough iron, you get **anemia,*** which can make you too tired to move. Not enough vitamin D or calcium causes bone problems. Worst of all,

***descendants**
(pronounce it like this)
dee-SEND-dents

***anemia**
(pronounce it like this)
ah-NEE-mee-ah

60

not enough vitamin C gives you **scurvy**! It's terrible! Your body aches, your bones break, your gums bleed, and *your teeth fall out*!

How could such a terrible thing happen to your ancestors? It was just a big genetic mistake, or what scientists call a bad **mutation**.

To be clear, mutations happen all the time, and they aren't always bad. Mutations are what cause the little differences between you and your friend. Mutations are what enable natural selection, with little differences adding up to big changes over time. But mutations can also make bigger differences. Maybe you've heard of someone with six fingers—that's a mutation. Or a completely white giraffe—an albino. That's a mutation too. Whether big or little, mutations happen deep inside the building blocks of your body, in something called your **DNA**.

Think of DNA as a cake recipe—each and every animal (including you) has its own unique recipe for making its own unique animal cake. But DNA is no ordinary cake recipe. It is a very, very, very, very complicated recipe with more than 20,000 ingredients, called **genes**.* And genes aren't ordinary ingredients—each gene is actually its own *separate* recipe organizing how different parts of you get made. Some genes control your hair color or how many teeth you have. Some genes work in teams; some work alone. And together these 20,000 genes combine in just such a way to make you the extraordinary and unique creature you are.

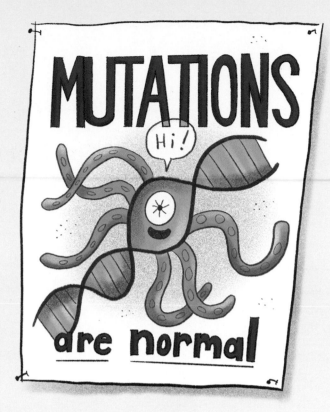

*gene
(pronounce it like this)
jeen

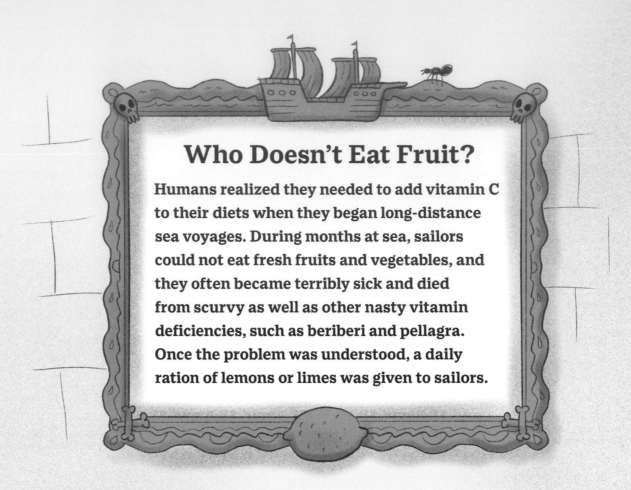

Who Doesn't Eat Fruit?

Humans realized they needed to add vitamin C to their diets when they began long-distance sea voyages. During months at sea, sailors could not eat fresh fruits and vegetables, and they often became terribly sick and died from scurvy as well as other nasty vitamin deficiencies, such as beriberi and pellagra. Once the problem was understood, a daily ration of lemons or limes was given to sailors.

Now, if you've ever followed a cake recipe, you know it's easy to make mistakes. You could forget the salt or use twice as much flour or add the wrong ingredients. Forget the salt, and the cake will be fine. Twice as much flour, the cake will be a rock. Add orange juice instead of milk, and you might discover something delicious. It's the same with mutations in your DNA. Mutations can be good or bad, they can do nothing at all, or they might be unexpectedly interesting and useful.

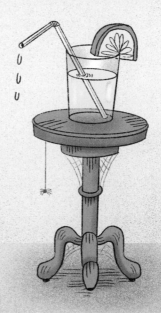

Washrooms

And so, long ago, a gene called GULO mutated in your monkey ancestors. GULO allows animals to make their own vitamin C. Once it broke, it could never be fixed. At the time, it didn't matter too much because those ancient monkeys ate fruit all day, every day. They got plenty of vitamin C from their diet. However, do you remember when I said that changes usually only stick around if they do something useful? Well, scientists think the GULO gene might also control how animals store fat. (Some genes do more than one thing.) Maybe the GULO break allowed your ancestors to fatten up. That would be useful for a monkey that never knows when it might see another banana, but not so useful for humans now that doughnuts have been invented.

Useful

Useless

Pardon me a moment.

I told you not to drink all that!

WRINKLY FINGERS

Ole Pruney

Carpolestes simpsoni
56.8 to 55.8 MYA | 4 ounces
Carpolestes lived in the Paleocene, after the Age of Dinosaurs. These primate-like creatures evolved opposable thumbs and big toes, perhaps to climb along branches to collect fruit.

IT HAPPENS TO EVERYONE.
When you're in the tub, your fingers and toes go pruney. No other part of you does this, and it doesn't happen to most other animals. So why does it happen to human fingers and toes? Nobody really knows, but some scientists think these wrinkles gave your ancestors a better grip on rainy days. Like the grooves on a tire, the wrinkles channeled water away, so fingers and toes could grasp wet branches without slipping.

You see, most tree-climbing animals have claws. But apes and monkeys have nails, like you. Nails can't dig into tree trunks like claws, but maybe nails help reach and pick the fruit growing at the bendy tips of branches, where claws wouldn't be as useful. Wrinkly Fingers and their nails may have given your ancestors a better grip on small, fruit-bearing branches. It's just a theory, but I think it's a good one.

And that brings us to the end of Your Inner Monkey. But we still have one final exhibit. The hero of all leftovers. To understand this one, we need to go back in time, way back…

Try This

◯ LOVE YOUR LEFTOVERS

How long does it take your fingers to go pruney?
Get a stopwatch. Do your friend's fingers take the same amount of time? And here is another test. You'll need marbles, a container with a small hole, and a large bucket of water. Your job is to put the marbles through the hole in the container, all underwater. Time yourself to see whether wrinkled fingers have better grip and work faster than unwrinkled fingers.

Juramaia sinensis
160 MYA | 3 inches
This tiny mouse-sized mammal was among the first to feed its growing babies inside its body with a placenta, the way you were fed inside your mother before you were born.

Thrinaxodon liorhinus aka the badger–iguana
245–240 MYA | 20 inches
Thrinaxodon was about the size of a house cat, lived in burrows, and may have had fur and whiskers.

Back before primates existed.

Back before mammals.

Archaeothyris florensis
306 MYA | 20 inches
This lizard-like creature was one of the first amniotes, which means it didn't need to lay its eggs in water, like amphibians. Its eggs had shells to survive on dry land.

Yes, we need to continue back in time—another 50 million years, to a time when your ancestors were still splashing about in water. We need to keep going back until we get to… Hiccups!

Back even before your ancestors were lizards.

HERO HICCUPS

aka Icky

Ichthyostega stensioei
365 MYA | 5 feet long
Ichthyostega was a large salamander-like creature. It mostly lived in shallow water, had lungs and gills, and may be an ancient ancestor (or at least an ancient cousin) of every bony creature that ever walked or slithered on land, including amphibians, lizards, birds, and mammals.

HICCUPS! Hiccups has true grit! The hero of all leftovers! Scientists think hiccups have been hanging around since your ancestors could breathe in the water *and* on the land. It's been about 350 million years since they could do that. See what I mean about true grit? Give Hiccups a standing ovation!

Let me explain with something less ancient, like a tadpole. As you might know, tadpoles live in water and look more like chubby fish than baby frogs. Like fish, they breathe underwater by sucking water into their mouths and forcing it out their **gills**—gills are the slits on the side of a fish's face. As tadpoles grow bigger and sprout legs, they also grow lungs. And this is where things get interesting. With gills *and* lungs, tadpoles need a way to close their air tube when underwater so they don't force water into their lungs (*blech! sputter!*) when they force water out their gills.

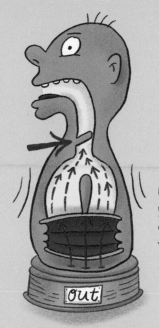

The diaphragm muscle spasms and causes the lungs to suck air in sharply. This sudden intake of air makes a flap in your throat snap shut.

in

out

For just a moment you can't breathe in or out, which causes you to make a "hic" sound.

To do this, tadpoles take a quick breath into their lungs and then squeeze their throats shut. Your ancestors did the same sort of thing to switch between air-breathing and underwater-breathing. And this air-suck-throat-squeeze muscle spasm is—you guessed it—Hiccups!

Why humans and most mammals still get hiccups 350 million years later is a bit of mystery. Some scientists think the *hic!* may be helpful for baby mammals to learn how to suck milk. Whatever the reason, Hiccups is my hero!

Babies growing inside their mothers hiccup a lot.

And they don't disappear! So that's something we *both* know about.

LOVE YOUR LEFTOVERS

Don't love your hiccups? Here are a few ideas to get rid of them: hold your breath, breathe into a paper bag, hug your knees tightly to your chest, pull on your tongue, drink icy water, eat a spoonful of honey, or suck on a lemon.

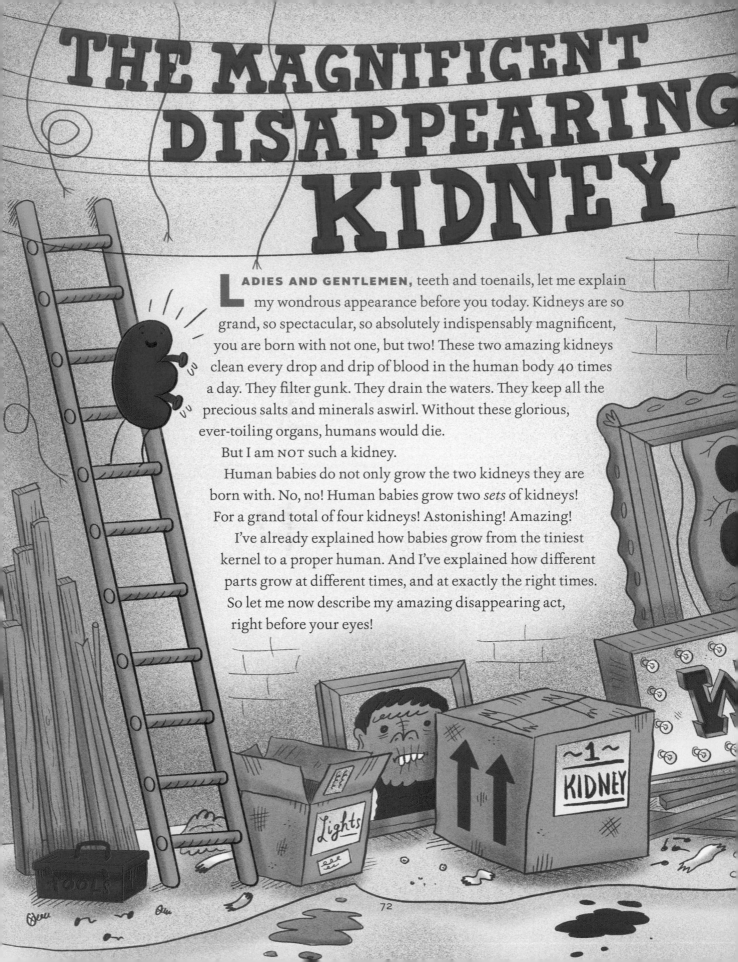

THE MAGNIFICENT DISAPPEARING KIDNEY

LADIES AND GENTLEMEN, teeth and toenails, let me explain my wondrous appearance before you today. Kidneys are so grand, so spectacular, so absolutely indispensably magnificent, you are born with not one, but two! These two amazing kidneys clean every drop and drip of blood in the human body 40 times a day. They filter gunk. They drain the waters. They keep all the precious salts and minerals aswirl. Without these glorious, ever-toiling organs, humans would die.

But I am NOT such a kidney.

Human babies do not only grow the two kidneys they are born with. No, no! Human babies grow two *sets* of kidneys! For a grand total of four kidneys! Astonishing! Amazing!

I've already explained how babies grow from the tiniest kernel to a proper human. And I've explained how different parts grow at different times, and at exactly the right times. So let me now describe my amazing disappearing act, right before your eyes!

We aren't as complex as the kidneys humans are born with, and we can't multitask like they do. We are ancient leftovers, but we are not useless. We toil! We labor! We have all the pluck and moxie of proper hardworking kidneys. You see, we work while human babies are building their second set of kidneys, the ones they will keep their whole lives. Babies could not build such complex, beautiful organs as the human kidney without us ancient kidneys working in the background, cleaning blood and filtering gunk, like the secret heroes we are. And then, once the second set is built and working fine, and just when you thought we could not possibly become any more charming, we vanish like magic. Voilà! All we leave behind are a few tubes with fancy names like the Wolffian duct and the epoöphoron as reminders of our glorious existence. We are leftovers! *And* we are important!

I have to admit, that's an impressive story.

Thank you. I know.

My friends, I'm sorry to say we have come to the end of the Museum of Odd Body Leftovers. I hope you have enjoyed your tour. And remember, this is only a tiny fraction of the miracles inside your body and only a glimpse of your extraordinary family of ancestors. There is so much more to learn and explore!

For now, please exit through the gift shop and buy a souvenir. Every cent goes toward keeping us leftovers and this museum open for business.

GLOSSARY

Achilles tendon
(*ah-KILL-lees TEN-don*)
the tissue connecting the calf muscle
to the heel.

amphibian
(*am-FIB-ee-uhn*)
a class of animals, including frogs, newts,
and salamanders, that can breathe in water
and on land.

ancestor
an older living thing from which more
recent ones are descended.

anemia
(*ah-NEE-mee-ah*)
a blood disorder, often caused by lack of iron.

bipedal
(*BAI-pee-dal*)
walking on two feet.

camouflage
(*CAM-oh-flahzh*)
a disguise designed to blend something
into the background.

coccyx
(*COK-sicks*)
a small triangular bone made from fused
vestigial bones at the bottom of the spine in
humans and some apes, also known as
a tailbone.

descendants
(*dee-SEND-dents*)
more recent living things related to older ones.

DNA (deoxyribonucleic acid)
genetic recipe (found in cells) that makes
each living thing unique.

evolution
the process by which all living things
develop and change from earlier forms.

fossils
preserved parts or impressions of a once-living
thing buried in rock from a past geological age.

gene
(*jeen*)
a segment of DNA. Genes carry the information
that controls which characteristics are passed
on from parent to child.

genetic variation
(*juh-NET-ic very-ay-shun*)
the differences between individuals of the
same species.

gill
an organ for breathing underwater
found in fish and some amphibians.

hominins
(*HOM-uh-nins*)
a group including all humans that ever
lived and all human-like ancestors.

lanugo
(*lah-NEW-go*)
soft hair that covers the body of some
newborns.

mammal
a member of a class of hairy animals that
nurse their young with milk.

milk teeth
a set of teeth that young mammals lose
as their permanent teeth grow in.

missing link
a gap in the fossil record, where scientists
aren't sure how an ancestor and its
descendants are related.

molars
large, flat teeth for serious chewing.

mutation
a change in DNA.

natural selection
a process by which life-forms that are better suited to their environment survive and have more offspring.

nictitating membranes
(*NICK-tuh-tay-ting MEM-brains*)
a transparent third eyelid that protects the eyeballs in some animals.

opposable toe
a big toe that can pinch together with the other toes in order to grasp things, the way a thumb does with fingers.

prosthetic
(*pross-THET-tic*)
artificial, describing a device that replaces a missing body part or helps a damaged one work better.

reflex
an automatic response in the body that happens in reaction to a particular event or action.

scurvy
a disease caused by not getting enough vitamin C.

sexual selection
a process of natural selection in which partners are chosen because of some attractive feature, like beautiful feathers.

species
(*SPEE-sees*)
a group of living things that are able to exchange genes and make more like themselves.

theropods
(*THER-uh-pods*)
an ancient group of animals that includes all living birds and a bunch of very fierce dinosaurs.

trait
a feature or characteristic controlled by a living thing's genes.

vestigial structures
(*ves-TIDGE-gee-al STRUCK-sures*)
body parts that appear to be useless now but were in some form once essential to a creature's ancestors.

wisdom teeth
the last adult teeth; a third set of molars at the back of the mouth often appearing in people's late teens or early 20s.

Human Tail!

FURTHER READING

Amazing Evolution: The Journey of Life by Anna Claybourne, illustrated by Wesley Robins (Ivy Kids, 2019)

Charles Darwin's On the Origin of Species adapted and illustrated by Sabina Radeva (Crown Books for Young Readers, 2019)

Head to Toe: My Body and How It Works by OKIDO (Thames & Hudson, 2012)

When We Became Humans: Our Incredible Evolutionary Journey by Michael Bright, illustrated by Hannah Bailey (words & pictures, 2019)

When Whales Walked: And Other Incredible Evolutionary Journeys by Dougal Dixon, illustrated by Hannah Bailey (words & pictures, 2018)

Try This

INDEX

This index is like a map, showing you where to find information inside this book. You can use it by looking for a subject that interests you, like "apes" or "dinosaurs" or "third eyelids." All of the main headings are in alphabetical order. The numbers after each key word are the page numbers where you will find information. Page numbers in a range (for example, 54–55) tell you that information is found on pages 54 *and* 55.

BIOS

RACHEL POLIQUIN writes about animals, mostly. She particularly likes celebrating unexpected heroes—the lumpy, lowly, and quietly extraordinary. She is the author of the Superpower Field Guide series, the Polite Predators series, and *The Strangest Thing in the Sea*. She lives in Vancouver, British Columbia, with her husband and three children.

CLAYTON HANMER (aka CTON) has illustrated several children's books, including *Trending: How and Why Stuff Gets Popular* and *Dog vs. Ultra Dog!* His award-winning comic art has also appeared in, among others, *National Geographic Kids*, the *New York Times*, and *Today's Parent*. He lives in Bloomfield, Ontario.

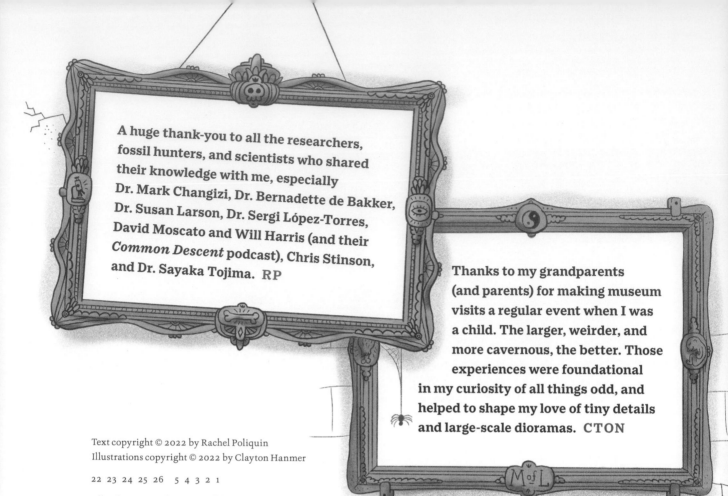

A huge thank-you to all the researchers, fossil hunters, and scientists who shared their knowledge with me, especially Dr. Mark Changizi, Dr. Bernadette de Bakker, Dr. Susan Larson, Dr. Sergi López-Torres, David Moscato and Will Harris (and their *Common Descent* podcast), Chris Stinson, and Dr. Sayaka Tojima. RP

Thanks to my grandparents (and parents) for making museum visits a regular event when I was a child. The larger, weirder, and more cavernous, the better. Those experiences were foundational in my curiosity of all things odd, and helped to shape my love of tiny details and large-scale dioramas. CTON

Text copyright © 2022 by Rachel Poliquin
Illustrations copyright © 2022 by Clayton Hanmer

22 23 24 25 26   5 4 3 2 1

Greystone Kids / Greystone Books Ltd.
greystonebooks.com

Cataloguing data available from Library and Archives Canada
ISBN 978-1-77164-745-8 (cloth)
ISBN 978-1-77164-746-5 (epub)

Canada

BRITISH COLUMBIA   BRITISH COLUMBIA ARTS COUNCIL
An agency of the Province of British Columbia

Canada Council   Conseil des arts
for the Arts   du Canada

MIX
Paper from responsible sources
FSC
www.fsc.org   FSC® C016973

Editing by Linda Pruessen
Copy editing by Dawn Loewen
Proofreading by Alison Strobel
Indexing by Stephen Ullstrom

Cover and interior design by Jessica Sullivan

Printed and bound in Singapore on FSC® certified paper at COS Printers Pte Ltd. The FSC® label means that materials used for the product have been responsibly sourced.

Greystone Books gratefully acknowledges the Musqueam, Squamish, and Tsleil-Waututh peoples on whose land our Vancouver head office is located.

Greystone Books thanks the Canada Council for the Arts, the British Columbia Arts Council, the Province of British Columbia through the Book Publishing Tax Credit, and the Government of Canada for supporting our publishing activities.